EIGHT DAYS (BACKWARDS)

Jeremy Dobrish

BROADWAY PLAY PUBLISHING INC
56 E 81st St., NY NY 10028-0202
212 772-8334 fax: 212 772-8358
http://www.BroadwayPlayPubl.com

EIGHT DAYS (BACKWARDS)
© Copyright 2004 by Jeremy Dobrish

First printing: April 2004
I S B N: 0-88145-229-7

Book design: Marie Donovan
Word processing: Microsoft Word for Windows
Typographic controls: Xerox Ventura Publisher 2.0 P E
Typeface: Palatino
Printed and bound in the U S A

ABOUT THE AUTHOR

Jeremy Dobrish is the Artistic Director of the critically acclaimed adobe theatre company which he co-founded in 1991. adobe's unique style has enabled it to become one of New York's most celebrated theater groups. Jeremy's plays for adobe include NOTIONS IN MOTION, THE HANDLESS MAIDEN, BLINK OF AN EYE, and ORPHEUS AND EURYDICE, all of which are published by Broadway Play Publishing Inc.

Off-Broadway directing credits include CLASS MOTHERS '68, starring Tony award winner Priscilla Lopez, THE COMPLETE WORKS OF WILLIAM SHAKESPEARE (ABRIDGED), and THE JOYS OF SEX (2002 N Y C Fringe award for excellence in directing). Other recent Off-Broadway directing credits include W P A, The Kirk, Soho Playhouse, and two seasons with the Young Playwrights Festival.

His directing credits for adobe include DUET! with Erin Quinn Purcell and Gregory Jackson, POONA and THE EIGHT both by Jeff Goode, as well as his own plays DECEPTION, ORPHEUS & EURYDICE, NOTIONS IN MOTION and BLINK OF AN EYE.

Jeremy has taught playwriting and directing workshops at Fordham, Washington Irving High School, and through Young Playwrights. He has spoken at N Y U, Wesleyan, Brown, the College of Staten Island, and Hofstra, and served on panels for ART/NY, The Dramatists Guild, the S D C Foundation, and The

Drama League. Jeremy is a member of the Dramatists Guild, S S D C, and the Vineyard Theater's Community of Artists.

EIGHT DAYS (BACKWARDS) opened on 16 June 2003 at the Vineyard Theater (Douglas Aibel, Artistic Director; Bardo S Ramírez, Managing Director; Jennifer Garvey-Blackwell, Executive Director, External Affairs). The cast and creative contributors were:

GLORIA/FORTUNE TELLER ....Randy Danson
FRANK/KAPLAN ....Bill Buell
CONSUELA/SELENA .... Daniella Alonso
MR GOLDBERG/BARTENDER ....Christopher Innvar
STERN/SHEILA GOLDBERG ....Barbara Garrick
WEINSTEIN/IZZY ....David Garrison
JONATHAN ....Josh Radnor

Director ....Mark Brokaw
Set design ....Mark Wendland
Costume design .... Michael Krass
Lighting design ....Mary Louis Geiger
Sound design ....Janet Kalas
Original music .... Lewis Flinn
Production manager .... Kai Brothers &Bridget Markov
Production stage manager ....Jennifer Rae Moore
Casting ....Cindy Tolan
Press representative ....Sam Rudy
General manager ....Rebecca Habel

CHARACTERS

GLORIA/FORTUNE TELLER, *female, 50s, in Scenes 1 &5*
FRANK/KAPLAN, *male, 50s, in Scenes 1, 3, 6 & 8*
CONSUELA/SELENA, *female, 20s, in Scenes 2, 4 & 6*
MR GOLDBERG/BARTENDER, *male, 40s, in Scenes 2, 4 & 7*
STERN/SHEILA GOLDBERG, *female, 40s, in Scenes 3, 6 & 7*
WEINSTEIN/IZZY, *male, 50s, in Scenes 3, 6 & 8*
JONATHAN, *male, 20s, in Scenes 4 & 5*

4 males, 3 females

A note about the doubling of actors: It's very important that when an actor plays the same character we know for certain that it's the same character, and when they play a different character we know for certain that it's a different character. Strong choices in costume, make-up, wigs as well as speech patterns and physicality are encouraged.

It might seem that it would be interesting to map out exactly how all of these characters interconnect, but ultimately I don't think it would be.

This play is meant to be performed without an intermission.

Scene One
A good boy

*(When Dolly speaks [which isn't often] her unheard
conversation is noted with a "/". She usually says little
more than a word.)*

(A restaurant table for two)

*(A title slide, placard, banner, or something: FRIDAY
(Today))*

*(The lights come up on a restaurant table for two set for
lunch. We sit and watch this lack of movement for a long
moment. At length GLORIA, a woman in her late fifties
dressed for a nice lunch, enters in a frenetic hurry and sits
down. Her head is buried in her purse. She doesn't seem to
notice that she is alone.)*

GLORIA: Oh God, Dolly, I'm so sorry I'm late. I've been
circling for..., I don't know how long. It's impossible
out there. Do you know what they say? That the
average parking space in New York City is available for
thirteen seconds. Thirteen, you believe that? I don't
know how you keep living in this Hell-hole. Suburbia is
the only life that makes sense to me anymore. *(She finds
and puts on her glasses.)* Ah, without these I'm useless.
(She buries her head in her menu.) Did you order already?
Like there's anything new I might have? Why do
people even look at menus at their favorite restaurants?
You always order the same thing no matter what right?
They do such a nice scampi here, why go with anything
else? *(She pauses. Seems to notice something disturbing.
Looks at the empty chair across from her.)* Dolly? *(She starts
rummaging through her purse in search of her cell phone.)* I

was so late, I was sure you'd be here.
I'm giving myself guilt for what? *(She hits speed dial.)*
/ Dolly? / Where the hell are you? / I'm at our place,
at our table, where should I be? / What? I called you
yesterday to reschedule. I left a message on your cell
phone thing. / What do you mean you didn't get it?
So you just sat there waiting for me? / How many
times did you call? / No I didn't. *(She looks at her
cellphone.)* Six messages. I hate these things. Dolly I'm
so sorry. / I can't believe you didn't get my message.
I went on and on about how I hate to reschedule our
Thursday lunches / well Consuela, you know the
Mexican I tutor, English as a second language literacy
volunteer program, my thing? / She rescheduled to
Thursday, to yesterday, but then it turns out anyway
that she cancelled on me. So I could have made it. /
Oh she had to change this with the that, and who the
hell knows with these people I can barely understand a
word anyway? But she's a sweetie, she really is. So now
what am I supposed to do? I have a story I'm dying to
tell you. / Something...special. Hold on, let me get my
plug, I'm gonna tell you a story, I'm not going to get the
brain cancer. *(She connects her earplug. This makes it seem
as though she is talking to herself, an effect which seems to
affect her as well.)* So Dolly, this story is going to knock
your socks off. *(She looks around conspiratorially to make
sure no one is eavesdropping on her.)* Alright. So Frank
says to me the other night, early last week, he says,

(We hear an amplified voice from offstage.)

FRANK: *(V O)* Gloria. We have to talk about something.

GLORIA: /I know. I'm thinking the same thing. Terrified
right? What is there a younger woman or something?
I mean this is Frank who doesn't say more than two
sentences a whole night of bridge other than "your
turn" and "is there more beer?". I mean with Mack and,
or Izzy it's a different thing, but add a woman into the

mix and it's bye-bye Frank. Unless he can help with something of course, and then it's all about, let me do that, do you know how this works?, let me tell you an interesting story about carburetors, I didn't marry him for his social skills. Anyway, what could he have to talk to me about that's so important it warrants an announcement like this? So my heart starts going you know, cause I'm afraid he's gonna ask for a divorce or something. I mean this can only be bad, right? / You know sometimes I forget how much I used to put him on a pedestal. So anyway, we sit on the couch, and I say something very polite and open given how tense I'm becoming, I say; "Yes, Frank, what is it you'd like to talk about?"

(Pause)

FRANK: *(V O)* I'd like to try S & M.

GLORIA: / I know. I was shocked too, so I said, and I'm keeping calm, I'm being very good, I said "what do you mean?"

FRANK: *(V O)* I'd like to serve a Mistress.

GLORIA: So I'm having these images in my head of some twenty-something sex Goddess in thigh-high patent leather boots with a whip and tits out to Teaneck. And I can't believe that my Frankie is saying this to me, you know? / So I say, "but Frank, I mean, I know things haven't been all that exciting between us lately, I mean we have been married twenty-five years, but that's no reason to go to a prostitute is it?"

FRANK: *(V O)* No, no, Gloria, no, you misunderstand, I want you to be my Mistress.

GLORIA: So now I'm having images of me in thigh-high patent leather boots and that's not a pretty sight, believe you me. / Oh you're sweet. Anyway, he starts blurting out in this jumbled mess of words, like he's

been thinking about this forever and now it's just
pouring out, all about how he wants to serve me, put
my needs first, submit to my whims. That he's tired
of being the decision maker all the time. He wants to
be out of control. He thinks it would turn him on. So
needless to say I am quite a bit sceptical. / I mean, well,
I guess I thought it sounded a little disgusting if you
want to know the truth. But he says to me that he read
this book, and he went to this store, and he thinks if I
read a little about it, maybe I would enjoy trying it with
him just once. And then he looks at me real close and he
says:

FRANK: *(V O)* It would mean a lot to me.

GLORIA: Dolly, in twenty-five years I don't think I've
ever heard him say that. Something he wants, he takes,
something he doesn't care about, he'll never care about.
But to give him something that would "mean a lot to
him"? This has me...I was going to say intrigued, but at
this point I might say confused. / O K. So he leaves the
book for me and I'm reading all about "scenes" and
"safewords" and "power switching" and God knows
what all, it's like a text book of kink or something.
And there are these sections that he's put little checks
next to you know, so to let me know that it particularly
interests him or something. And a couple of days later
he leaves me a note that says:

FRANK: *(V O)* Mistress Gloria, on Friday night I would
like to be your slave.

GLORIA: First of all "Mistress Gloria" I mean, I don't
know whether to laugh, cry or run for the hills. But it
was that he left me a note. That he couldn't talk to me
about this. After twenty-five years, and here's a thing
my husband can't say to me. What is this? Where is this
in him? / Men is right. So what do I do? I leave him a
note. "Alright slave, Friday after Consuela". Because
of course Consuela is usually Friday except yesterday

when it was supposed to be Thursday but wasn't.
So this is a week ago Wednesday and, Dolly I have to
tell you, the next two days are very strange. It's like
nothing at all is happening between us that's out of the
ordinary, but of course underneath everything we say
or do, there's this nervous energy. Especially from
Frank. He can barely look me in the eye. He's like a
little kid all of a sudden. So anyway last Friday comes,
a week ago today, and I go to see Consuela, and Dolly,
I cannot keep my mind on track. She's "*como esta-ing*"
this, and I'm "Johnny wants to go to the beach that",
and she's being her usual sweet and timid self, but I
mean all I can think about is what is this going to be
like? / I'm... well I was a little scared. But definitely
by this point I would have to say intrigued. So I come
home from after Consuela and what do I see? / First of
all: candles, all over the house. On both floors. In every
room. And Frank hates candles. He'd as soon use the
wick as dental floss. Next: Rose petals, strewn on the
floor like a living red carpet, and the *piece de resistance*?
/ Frank himself. Prepare yourself. He is dressed like
this:

(FRANK *enters. He is a man in his late fifties. Could be a bit
heavy. Maybe balding. He is dressed in high heels, stockings,
a black, shiny, rubbery dress and an apron. He stands in
a separate area where he will remain, standing somewhat
impassively, not acting out the actions described but speaking
with the suitable emotions.)*

GLORIA: I can't believe what I'm seeing. I mean this is
my Frank. Mister no fuss, no attention, fade into the
background. He looks about as ridiculous as a human
male could possibly look. / But he has this sincerity
splashed across his entire face. Like all he wants to do is
be accepted. And. Or taken seriously. So he comes over
to me, takes my coat, puts down my pocket book, and

kneels at my feet. He takes my hand and kisses it.
And from his knees he looks up at me and says:

FRANK: Mistress Gloria, beautiful shining star, how
may I serve you?

GLORIA: How may he serve me? I could only think of
one thing. "Get me a drink... Slave." And he gets up,
scampers to his feet and runs to prepare me a drink.
You should've seen him. I haven't seen him move this
fast in years. And in heels no less. Am I shocking you?
/ Good cause it gets worse. So he brings me the drink
and kneels at my feet again. And I say "Thank you
slave. You are a good slave." And the words feel so
funny in my throat, but he's looking up at me like a
little puppy and he says:

(GLORIA *wells up with emotion as they say this together.*)

FRANK & GLORIA: Oh Mistress Gloria, beautiful shining
star, you are the most beautiful Mistress a lucky slave
like me could ever ask for.

GLORIA: And that hits me hard. And suddenly that
twenty-something sex kitten with tits to Teaneck has
nothing on me. I mean, I am feeling good. I am feeling
sexy, and strong, and confident,and powerful, and...
in love.

FRANK: Mistress Gloria, beautiful, shining star, how
may I serve you next?

GLORIA: So I see how he's dressed and I say, "Well
slave, I think the tub could use a good scrubbing" And
he runs. Runs. To the utility sink. He pulls out the latex
gloves, the Ajax, the sponge, I didn't think he knew
where the Ajax was. And he runs up to the bathroom
wobbling in his high heels, the whole time yelling:

FRANK: I will please my Mistress. Whatever you
command. I will please you.

GLORIA: And then he hands me this...paddle type thing that he must've gotten from wherever he got that crazy dress and he says:

FRANK: If I do not please you, Mistress. If I do not move fast enough, or do a good enough job, you must punish me.

GLORIA: And he gets on his hands and knees, in stockings and high heels mind you, and starts scrubbing the tub. Dolly, in twenty-five years he has never, ever, lifted a finger to help clean the bathroom. And he is being so fast, and so thorough. And I'm just standing there sipping my drink. And he's scrubbing. And he's scrubbing. And he's scrubbing. And he says again:

FRANK: If I am not moving fast enough or doing a good enough job, you must punish me Mistress.

GLORIA: I mean, I don't see how he can move any faster. I don't want him to throw his back out again. And then I realize he wants me to punish him. That's part of the game. So I say "you must move faster slave" and I give him a little paddle on his behind. I mean I could barely bring myself to spank the kids, how the hell am I supposed to paddle Frank? But he says to me, he actually says:

FRANK: If it would please my Mistress, your slave would like it a little harder.

GLORIA: So Dolly..., I slap his ass! / I mean, I'm sorry, but I just don't know how else to put it. He's scrubbing, and I'm slapping, and he's yelling:

FRANK: Thank you Mistress, I will scrub faster.

GLORIA: And he's scrubbing faster, and I'm slapping harder, and I'm thinking to myself: this is for twenty-five years of never doing this, this is for twenty-five years of your needs coming first, and you want to know something Dolly? It felt good. / Watching his ass turn red, it felt sexy. Having that power. And it felt good to him too, whatever atoning he was doing, or whatever it was, I know it did because I start to realize that while he scrubs, and while he gets slapped, he is... rubbing himself up against the floor of the tub. And at first I think that's weird, and then I think, well geez, I'd kind of like to be rubbing myself too, so I say "Slave. How dare you rub yourself against the tub." And he's pleading:

FRANK: No Mistress, I was not.

GLORIA: "Do not lie to me slave, how dare you. You may only have pleasure at the whim of your Mistress." That was a line I read in the book. And he jumps out of the tub, and begins kissing my shoes, apologizing profusely. And I say "make it up to me slave. You must give me the ultimate pleasure".

FRANK: Yes Mistress, of course Mistress, anything you say Mistress.

GLORIA: So he leads me to the bedroom. Lays me down on the bed. And he...puts his head between my legs. Dolly he has not done this in...I don't know, twenty years. He was always...unwilling. But he starts and Dolly...he is terrible. Like a cat licking up milk. Up and down and up and down. And so I start to let my mind wander as I do when he...goes through his sexual routines, and just as I do, he stops. And he looks up at me and says:

FRANK: Mistress, I only want to please you. If I am not doing this right, please help me.

GLORIA: The man is almost sixty. So I help him. I say a little higher. A little harder. a little slower. And Dolly, he gives me a "yowza". I mean yow-za. I have not had a "yowza" in...I can't even count how long. And when I am finished. Not when he is finished, but when I am

finished, he takes me to the freshly scrubbed tub, with
the candles still burning, and he washes me. And he
puts little kisses on me and dries me, and powders me.
And he brings me back to bed and lays in my arms, his
head on my breast, and he says:

(FRANK and GLORIA look at each other for the first time.)

FRANK: Did I do alright? Did I please you Mistress
Gloria? Am I a good boy?

GLORIA: And I say yes Frank. ...More than alright...
You pleased me very much.

(Lights fade to black.)

Scene Two
A mutually beneficial business arrangement

*(Note: CONSUELA is Hispanic, and changes her English
proficiency to suit the moment.)*

*(MR GOLDBERG's bedroom. A bed. A night table with a
phone and clock on it. On one side of the bed is a pile of
hastily discarded clothing: a man's suit, on the other side,
a dress. MR GOLDBERG has a lot of money and it shows.)*

*(A title slide, placard, banner or something: THURSDAY
(yesterday))*

*(MR GOLDBERG lays under the covers of his bed, sleeping
although it is the middle of the day. Laying next to him,
awake, is CONSUELA. She sits, thinking, sad. Perhaps a
tear falls. She looks at the clock by the bed.)*

CONSUELA: *(Under her breath)* Dios mio!

*(CONSUELA quickly gets out of the bed, careful not to wake
MR GOLDBERG. She puts on the dress on the floor. She is
heading for the door as MR GOLDBERG stirs.)*

MR GOLDBERG: Hmm? Sheila? *(He awakes and sees* CONSUELA.*)* Oh. Right. Hi baby. What time is it?

*(*CONSUELA *speaks with a thick accent.)*

CONSUELA: It's one, I have to go.

MR GOLDBERG: Go? No, stay.

CONSUELA: I have my tutor.

MR GOLDBERG: Don't go, come on. Let's do it again. I'm up, look.

*(*MR GOLDBERG *raises the sheets to show* CONSUELA *his erection.)*

CONSUELA: Mr Goldberg, *por favor. (She puts her hair up.)*

MR GOLDBERG: Jesus Christ, look at you. How old are you Consuela?

CONSUELA: Twenty two.

MR GOLDBERG: Twenty fucking two. Hallelujah.

CONSUELA: *Como?*

MR GOLDBERG: Do you know what I was like when I was twenty two?

CONSUELA: Mr Goldberg...

MR GOLDBERG: Sit down Consuela.

CONSUELA: I have to....

MR GOLDBERG: Sit down!

(She sits.)

MR GOLDBERG: Twenty two? Let's see. Just graduated. Living in New York on a hundred and tenth street, and this is before all the fucking yuppies took over. One bedroom piece of shit walk up, sending half of my nothing paycheck to my Mother who, since my father died, is a raging alcoholic, putting myself through N Y U business school and do you want to know what?

CONSUELA: What?

MR GOLDBERG: With all that I have now, with all that I have, I was about ten times happier then. Do you understand?

CONSUELA: If you let me go, my English will be more good and I can understand you better.

MR GOLDBERG: Don't play naive with me, you understand every word. You're a smart girl, Consuela, you'll go far. I know. I can smell it in people. You're not going to be my maid forever. You know that right?

CONSUELA: Mr Goldberg, I have to go, Mrs. Gloria gets very angry when I'm late.

MR GOLDBERG: Call her, tell her you're not coming.

CONSUELA: I have to learn my English.

MR GOLDBERG: Your English is fine, It's about ten times better than Daniel's and he's almost done with high school, fucking apathetic, life-wasting moron. Do you know what a preposition is?

CONSUELA: A what?

MR GOLDBERG: Well neither do I! Now call Mrs Whatever and tell her you're very sorry, but you'll see her next week. I'm not at work, and my work is important.

(CONSUELA *goes to the phone.*)

MR GOLDBERG: No. Here. *(He pulls a cell phone from his blazer pocket.)* Use this. I have free minutes I need to use.

(CONSUELA *takes the phone and pushes some buttons. She holds it to her ear.*)

CONSUELA: Mrs Gloria. *Hola. Como estas?* I mean, "hello", "how are you"? Oh good. I having a difficult today. I can't come for the English. Juan has a sick and I have to stay. *Como?* Well I'm sorry you change your lunch. O K. He'll be O K. Thank you very much, Mrs Gloria. *Lo siento. Gracias.* Bye-bye. She hands the phone to Mr Goldberg who hangs it up.

MR GOLDBERG: How is Juan anyway?

CONSUELA: He's O K.

MR GOLDBERG: And the other one? What's his name?

CONSUELA: Miguel.

MR GOLDBERG: Still in Mexico?

CONSUELA: *Si.*

MR GOLDBERG: He's O K?

CONSUELA: Mr Goldberg, if you want to do it again, let's do it again, if not, I have other things to do.

(MR GOLDBERG *raises a hand to* CONSUELA. CONSUELA *flinches.*)

MR GOLDBERG: How fucking dare you? I am your... well, your employer. You do not speak to me like that. Do you want me to report you to immigration little miss no-greencard?

CONSUELA: I'm sorry.

MR GOLDBERG: I ask you a question about your sick child. I show concern, compassion for you and you sass back at me?

CONSUELA: I'm sorry. He's fine. He's O K. He's better.

MR GOLDBERG: Good. I'm glad to hear that.

CONSUELA: O K.

MR GOLDBERG: I'm sorry I....

CONSUELA: O K.

MR GOLDBERG: That was wrong. I'm sorry. But you should show respect.

CONSUELA: O K.

MR GOLDBERG: Alright. Are you alright?

CONSUELA: Alright.

(The phone rings.)

MR GOLDBERG: Oh for fuck's...

CONSUELA: Should I...?

MR GOLDBERG: Answer it.

CONSUELA: If it's Mrs Goldberg, she'll know I should be at Mrs Gloria's for my English.

MR GOLDBERG: Mrs Goldberg's been in Seattle since Saturday. It's barely ten there. If she's even out of bed yet, she's probably shopping with her sister or otherwise forgetting about me. Answer it.

(She does.)

CONSUELA: Goldberg residence. Mr Goldberg? No. He's not here. Who is calling? John Winston?

MR GOLDBERG: John Winston? Weinstein? John Weinstein? *(He grabs the phone.)* Weinstein, hey what's up, just walked in. No I couldn't make it today I'm still dealing with Sheila's thing. Hmm? Yeah, she is in Seattle. If only that meant she didn't need all my attention twenty four seven right? So how'd yesterday's meeting end up? Hate to miss those Wednesday noon meetings. You missed me? Yeah, sure we can do a face to face. You want to do lunch tomorrow? Hang on a second, let me get my pilot. *(He pulls a palm pilot from his blazer on the floor.)* Hang on, just getting the calendar up. Go to. Friday. Hang on. What time? One. Lunch with Weins-s- not B, S. Hang on. -stein. E-I-N. N. N. Good. Usual place? See you then. Ciao. *(He hangs up.)* That, Consuela, is very good news. That, is in all likelihood a well deserved, long overdue, promotion. And that fucker Kaplan said "watch my back", the fuck does he know? There's nothing worse than fake concern and compassion. But see that's what I admire about you. To you, all of life is business. It's all one big business transaction. If I could do that... Well. Anyway. Let's celebrate. You like champagne?

CONSUELA: *Como?*

MR GOLDBERG: Champagne? You like...? Of course you like champagne. Be right back.

(MR GOLDBERG exits. Perhaps the lights shift a bit. CONSUELA sits for a moment. Contemplates the cell phone and pilot. Pretends to dial numbers on the cell phone. Her English is suddenly much better.)

CONSUELA: Boop-boop-boop-boop-boop. Hello Winesucker you old fuck. What? Oh no, I'm just here fucking my maid to take care of my wife. At least this time I didn't cry from all the guilt so things are looking up. How was the meeting? Buy. Sell. Fuck. Hold on let me get my pilot. *(She pretends to write in the pilot.)* Lunch. Meeting. Meet with everyone and fuck them. Hold on, I can't spell my own name. By the way, did I ever tell you about my life when I was young? I was a privileged white man with every advantage, but I like to pretend it was hard. I don't even know what "hard" means. Just look at my dick. *(She pretends to hang up but speaks at the phone.)* One day Freddie will come back like a thief in the night. He'll see what you do to me. He'll piss down your throat, gut you like the pig you are, and serve your heart to the dogs.

(She puts everything back as the lights shift back. MR GOLDBERG re-enters with two glasses of champagne.)

MR GOLDBERG: I know it's a little early in the day for the bubbly, but a promotion's a promotion. And right now I'd much rather get drunk and climb on top of you than call Sheila and get belittled and berated. Bottoms up.

(They drink. He quickly, she slowly.)

MR GOLDBERG: You think I'm not a good husband am I right? Because of the things I say. Well I am a good husband. Hell, I took Sheila to the airport on Saturday myself God damn it. No fucking car service. Took her right to the gate, sixteen hundred and four bucks for a first class ticket straight down the toilet. And that's devotion whether she sees it or not. And I'm certainly a hell of a lot better than your dead beat husband who left you. With two kids. Where is he now? A good man does not leave his family. A good man keeps his family together and that is what I do and I am a good man. And a good husband. I do what I have to do to keep my marriage together. Period. And you want to know something, Consuela? Having sex with you is when I feel the most alive. The most...powerful. Really. I mean that as a compliment. I mean, if you don't enjoy fucking, then what the hell is there? What's left? I need you. I do. Without you, life would be...just... grey. He reaches into his pants pocket and removes his wallet. He takes out two hundred dollar bills.

CONSUELA: Mr Goldberg.

MR GOLDBERG: Look at me, Consuela. I know you're not a prostitute. And you know you're not a prostitute. But me leaving extra money in your envelope each time we...it's just silly. We both know what we're doing. We have a mutually beneficial...business arrangement. Take it. Just take it.

(She doesn't.)

MR GOLDBERG: Oh for God's sake take it. I know you need it.

(Reluctantly, she takes the money.)

MR GOLDBERG: What do you do with it all anyway? You're making a small fortune off me. Hmmm?

CONSUELA: I send it to my sister. In Mexico. For Miguel.

MR GOLDBERG: Your little one?

CONSUELA: *Si.*

MR GOLDBERG: Is he alright? I worry about him.

CONSUELA: Mr Goldberg, I don't want to talk about it.

MR GOLDBERG: I'm just asking is he ok? Jesus, it's not a big deal. Just tell me he's O K.

CONSUELA: He's O K.

MR GOLDBERG: Good. I'm glad.

(CONSUELA is obviously upset. Maybe crying)

MR GOLDBERG: What? What is it? What's wrong?

CONSUELA: Miguel.

MR GOLDBERG: You miss him?

CONSUELA: His heart. His heart is so big. But it's no good. It beats. Boom, boom-boom- boom. Boom, boom-boom-boom. Too many times. He will not be alive much longer.

MR GOLDBERG: It's a wonderful thing you do. Come here. *(He takes* CONSUELA *in his arms.)* To come to New York. To work. To send money to your son. You're a noble woman Consuela and that's what I've been saying. It's so clear. It shines through your skin. It's in your cheeks. Your eyes. You're so beautiful.

(He goes to kiss her. She resists. He is more forceful. She still resists.)

MR GOLDBERG: Consuela.

(He reaches into his wallet. Pulls out another hundred and sets it on the table. He goes to kiss her. She relents. He gets on top of her, rubbing himself against her and moaning softly as she cries to herself. Lights fade to black.)

Scene Three
Workday

(WEINSTEIN is a businessman. STERN is a business woman, tough. KAPLAN should be played as young as possible.)

(This scene should move very quickly.)

(A conference room. A beautiful table. Four fancy chairs. a speakerphone on the table. Two men in suits, and a woman in a sexy power suit sit around the table with pens, notepads, etc.)

(A title slide, placard, banner or something: WEDNESDAY (The day before yesterday))

(Tableaux: STERN, WEINSTEIN and KAPLAN sit around the table. Waiting. Anxious. Sit in this for a long beat then lights up.)

STERN: What time is it?

WEINSTEIN: 12:15.

KAPLAN: You don't wear a watch?

STERN: That fucker. What?

WEINSTEIN: You want to start?

KAPLAN: You don't wear a...? How do you know what time it is?

STERN: People tell me what time it is. You have a problem with that?

KAPLAN: I was just asking. Hey, what do you call a watch with no hands?

WEINSTEIN: It's 12:15 if you want to....

STERN: We can't start without Goldberg. He's got all the....

KAPLAN: Digitless!

STERN: How can we start without him? What's the point?

WEINSTEIN: He isn't here. We have to start.

STERN: So unbelievably disrespectful.

KAPLAN: My wife always keeps me waiting.

STERN: There's three of us, he's late by fifteen minutes, that's like he's forty five minutes late. Forty five minutes of our collective wasted time. He could call right? He has a fucking cell phone. He could call here. He could call my cell phone. Jane Stern. Call me. Why do we have cell phones if we don't use them to call when we're going to be late?

WEINSTEIN: You want me to page him?

STERN: No, Weinstein. I want him to be here. Why is he not here?

WEINSTEIN: He's not here.

STERN: I want him to be here.

WEINSTEIN: Well, he's not here. So you want to start, or you want me to page him?

STERN: Page him.

(WEINSTEIN *picks up the phone and dials.* KAPLAN *picks up* STERN's *cell phone and examines it.* WEINSTEIN *punches in his number over the following.)*

KAPLAN: Is this that new one from Motorola?

STERN: Yes.

KAPLAN: Does it have that thing...?

STERN: Yes.

KAPLAN: That is so fucking cool.

(WEINSTEIN *hangs up.)*

WEINSTEIN: I paged him. Let's start.

STERN: We can't start without him.

KAPLAN: I feel like I'm in Waiting For Godot. "Nothing to be done."

STERN: Shut up Gary.

WEINSTEIN: We have a lot we have to get through.

STERN: I have a 1:30.

WEINSTEIN: So, right, so let's start.

KAPLAN: He's kind of a fuck up.

WEINSTEIN: He is not a fuck up.

KAPLAN: No, I'm just saying. Lately I mean. He's a great guy, absolutely, but what's up with him?

WEINSTEIN: He's not a fuck up.

KAPLAN: No. Just lately. Hasn't he been fucking up lately?

STERN: He has been fucking up lately.

KAPLAN: He has. That's all I'm saying. I told him "watch your back".

WEINSTEIN: What's your point?

KAPLAN: No, just, you think everything's O K? At home? His family? Whatever? I'm just saying is all.

STERN: Well I don't give a fuck. He's having problems at home? Who doesn't have problems? You have a noon meeting, you're there at eleven forty five. You're not there at eleven forty five, you make a fucking phone call! We meet every Wednesday at noon. This is not breaking news.

KAPLAN: Are you ok? Is everything alright with you at home?

(The speakerphone buzzes. A voice is heard.)

VOICE: Mr Goldberg. Line one.

(WEINSTEIN *picks up the phone.*)

WEINSTEIN: Hello? Where are you? She is? Is everything alright? Yes, we're sorry too. O K, we'll just do it without you. No, no problem, it's ok, it's just that you have the.... just give me the numbers...hold on. Go. *(He picks up a pen and jots down some figures.)* Uh-huh. Uh-huh. Right. That bad, huh? O K. No. We'll be fine. You make sure Sheila's O K. We'll page you if we have questions and the summary'll be on your e-mail by five. O K. Right. Bye. *(He hangs up.)*

STERN: He's not coming?

WEINSTEIN: He's not coming. Let's start.

STERN: What do you mean he's not coming?

WEINSTEIN: His wife's having another episode.

STERN: Episode of what?

WEINSTEIN: She has a thing.

KAPLAN: What's bad?

WEINSTEIN: Her thing?

KAPLAN: On the phone, you said "that bad"

WEINSTEIN: He gave me the numbers.

STERN: They're that bad?

WEINSTEIN: They're not good.

STERN: Let me see.

(WEINSTEIN *turns the pad to her.*)

STERN: Fuck!

KAPLAN: Let me see.

(WEINSTEIN *turns the pad to him.*)

KAPLAN: Ouch.

STERN: That fucker.

WEINSTEIN: It's not that bad.

STERN: His wife has a thing?

WEINSTEIN: She gets this...it's happened before.

STERN: He comes in here with those numbers, he goes home unemployed. Suddenly his wife has a thing? This man does not understand his job.

WEINSTEIN: Oh come on.

STERN: We can't show those. How the fuck are we supposed to show those?

WEINSTEIN: It's not that bad.

STERN: Are you on crack? Kaplan are these bad?

KAPLAN: Bad.

STERN: We're supposed to be up thirty percent. We're down...what? Twelve?

WEINSTEIN: It was a difficult quarter. You project high, you're bound to fall short sometimes. That's life. It's like in a relationship, if you expect too much, or the wrong thing...

STERN: Oh, please don't give me a fucking lecture on relationships.

WEINSTEIN: Well, why do we project so high when we know we won't make it?

STERN: We do not project high and we did not fall short. We made a calculated estimate and something unforseen has temporarily caused a dip. But we are not down. Do you understand that we cannot show that? I will not show that. I will not get fired. I need some creative accounting and he gives me down twelve.

WEINSTEIN: Well, it's the truth.

STERN: The truth? Hey. I'd love to show "the truth". Just give me a different truth to show. I have a responsibility to this job. I care. I show up. And I need to be up, his numbers need to be up and if he is going to continue to be unwilling to cooperate....

(WEINSTEIN *picks up the phone.*)

WEINSTEIN: I'm paging him.

KAPLAN: Isn't his wife out of town?

WEINSTEIN: You want to see what he can do with the numbers, he has the numbers. I'm paging him.

KAPLAN: I thought she was.

STERN: He should be here.

WEINSTEIN: He should be here. He's not here. He has the numbers. He'll call back, and he'll tell us if there's anything we can do. O K? Until then we wait. O K?

(*Pause*)

KAPLAN: "Nothing to be done."

STERN: Gary.

(*Pause*)

KAPLAN: Have you guys seen those new Sony laptops? What's his name upstairs has one. Fucking light as a feather.

WEINSTEIN: Ooh.

STERN: What?

WEINSTEIN: I just had the strangest *deja vu*.

KAPLAN: God!!!

WEINSTEIN: What?

KAPLAN: I hate that!

WEINSTEIN: Deja vu?

KAPLAN: Scares the bejesus out of me. I mean: what is it?

(Pause)

STERN: I hate this job.

(Pause. The speakerphone buzzes. A voice is heard.)

VOICE: Mrs Kaplan. Line one.

STERN: What? Fuck. No.

KAPLAN: Tell her I'll call her back.

STERN: Where the fuck is he? He's by his pager two minutes ago. Fucking call back.

WEINSTEIN: You want me to page him again?

STERN: You just fucking paged him. I want him to call.

(The speakerphone buzzes. A voice is heard.)

VOICE: Mrs Kaplan. Line one. She says it's important.

STERN: Oh for fuck's sake.

(KAPLAN picks up the phone.)

KAPLAN: Hi Barbara, what's up? I'm just in a meeting here, what's up? Well, no, I don't mean to be brusque, I'm just in the middle of something, what's up? What? Sure. Hold on, let me get...you know if I don't write it down...uh-huh, uh-huh, sure. You couldn't have left this on my voice mail? No, of course I like to talk to you too, it's just...O K. We'll discuss it later, O K? Uh-huh. I don't...I don't want to...I love you too. *(He hangs up.)*

STERN: Fucking quart of milk?

KAPLAN: She's my wife.

STERN: I'm in charge of a team. This one has a wife who interrupts progress report meetings because she needs milk. My numbers guy can't make it in because his wife has a thing, an episodic thing. How 'bout you Weinstein? You gonna tell me you have to stay home from work tomorrow because your wife has her fucking period?

WEINSTEIN: I'm like you. Married to my job...

STERN: That's what I like to hear.

WEINSTEIN: Unfortunately. Still. And my wife died five years ago and I'd appreciate it if you...

STERN: Oh, I'm sorry, you wear a ring so I thought...

(WEINSTEIN *removes his wedding band and shoves it in his pocket.*)

WEINSTEIN: Can't a man just wear a ring? Does it have to mean something? I mean, Jesus Christ, you don't know the first thing about us.

STERN: I beg your pardon, but I know plenty.
(*To* KAPLAN) You have a son right? Who I met?

KAPLAN: I have three kids.

STERN: You do? Well how many have I met?

KAPLAN: I don't know.

STERN: But the one I met, good looking boy.

KAPLAN: Jonathan.

STERN: Going places. Just graduated right?

KAPLAN: Two years ago.

STERN: He's a...what is he?

KAPLAN: Not much at the moment.

STERN: Exactly. See?

WEINSTEIN: He's a great kid.

STERN: Suddenly we're talking about kids?

WEINSTEIN: Great at whatever he puts his mind to.

STERN: Can we please get back on the....

WEINSTEIN: What's he up to these days?

KAPLAN: Called me late last night actually. I think he'd had a few. I think he'd been crying. Asked me if his mother and I were soul mates.

WEINSTEIN: What did you tell him?

KAPLAN: I told him....

(Pause)

KAPLAN: *(To* STERN*)* You are a bitch.

STERN: Excuse me?

KAPLAN: So she called me? So what? We're sitting here waiting. Did I get in someone's way?

STERN: I'm a what?

KAPLAN: I can't tell my wife I love her? For what?

STERN: I'm a bitch? I'm efficient. A leader. Fuck you.

KAPLAN: I don't think I'm the one who needs to get fucked.

STERN: I beg your pardon.

KAPLAN: Married to your work? Is that what you said? As if that could replace something.

STERN: Men can't handle me. They get threatened. They can't take it.

KAPLAN: Who would want to take it?

STERN: Get the fuck out of this office. You're fired. I will not be spoken to like that. I am the leader of this team. Apologize, or get the fuck out.

KAPLAN: You can't just fire people.

STERN: Watch me. You're fired, Kaplan. I've got fifty overqualified resumes on my desk. Weinstein fire Goldberg.

KAPLAN: What is this the New Jew Revue in here?

WEINSTEIN: Oh come on.

STERN: I'm serious. Tomorrow he goes. Take him to lunch, do a face to face if it'll make you feel better, but I need someone who will fucking give me up not down!

KAPLAN: This is no way to run a team. Inspire us when you hire us, don't fire us.

STERN: Thank you, Jesse Jackson.

KAPLAN: Do you have any love? Anywhere in your life? Do you?

STERN: I love my job.

KAPLAN: You hate your job.

STERN: Didn't I fire you?

WEINSTEIN: Why don't we all take a deep breath and start this meeting over?

(Everyone stops. Long pause. Everyone looks at each other as they steep in their resentment. Finally:)

KAPLAN: I'm sorry.

STERN: Apology accepted.

KAPLAN: And don't you have something you'd like to say?

STERN: What are we in third grade?

WEINSTEIN: Just say you're sorry. You don't have to mean it. Just say it so we can get on with this.

STERN: My family's not dysfunctional enough? Now I have to put up with you people? If Goldberg were here, we could have had our meeting, we could have stayed out of each other's way, everything would have been fine.

WEINSTEIN: He's not here! Jesus Fucking Christ!! He's not here!!! Will you deal with what is?

VOICE: Mr Goldberg. Line one.

(They look at each other.)

(Blackout)

Scene Four
Last night on earth

(A dimly lit bar)

(A title slide, placard, banner or something: TUESDAY (The day before))

(SELENA sits at the bar wearing a tight mini skirt. The bartender is selling a joke to her.)

BARTENDER: So the octopus looks at the bagpipe and says, "play it? If I can figure out how to get it's clothes off, I'm gonna fuck it."

(SELENA doesn't laugh.)

BARTENDER: Oh come on, you don't think that's funny?

SELENA: I guess I'm just not in a very funny mood. Sorry.

(JONATHAN enters looking very harried. He looks around frantically. He sees SELENA. This calms him. He smiles and approaches the bar.

JONATHAN: *(To the bartender)* What time is it?

BARTENDER: 11:45

JONATHAN: Shit.

BARTENDER: Get you something?

JONATHAN: Uh, sure.

BARTENDER: What would you like?

JONATHAN: Wh...? Oh, beer.

BARTENDER: We have Heine....

JONATHAN: Whatever.*(To* SELENA*)* Hi. *(No response)*
Do you believe in love at first sight?

SELENA: Oh please.

JONATHAN: It's not a pick up line I swear. Well,
maybe it is. But not like normal. Do you?

SELENA: I really don't want to talk to anybody. O K?
Nothing personal.

JONATHAN: What about, not love at first sight, but more
like a soul mate?

SELENA: I'm really not interested ok?

JONATHAN: I'm just asking if...

SELENA: Look are you going to stop talking to me or am
I going to have to move?

JONATHAN: You don't need to be hostile. It's a simple
question.

SELENA: No, I do need to be hostile. I'm in a bad mood.
I'm not usually hostile, but right now I don't want to
talk to you. Am I being unclear?

JONATHAN: What happened?

SELENA: I am being unclear. Fuck off. Is that more clear?

JONATHAN: Why are you in a bad mood?

SELENA: Is there anything I can say that will get you to
leave me alone?

JONATHAN: No. It's 11:47. Eight. No.

SELENA: You turn into a pumpkin at midnight?

JONATHAN: No.

SELENA: Lose a bet if you don't get laid?

JONATHAN: No. I just feel like this is my last night on earth. I woke up this morning convinced and I've spent the whole day looking.

(BARTENDER *delivers the beer.*)

BARTENDER: Four dollars. And if the lady doesn't feel like talking, why don't you give her a break?

JONATHAN: Just talk to me. Look, I have fifteen minutes left or, what like eleven, ten minutes. It's not gonna kill you.

SELENA: Fine. Ten minutes. Then you'll leave me alone? Fine. What would you like to talk about?

JONATHAN: Why are you in such a bad mood?

SELENA: Can't we start with the weather. How bout those Knicks? What do you do?

JONATHAN: Sure. Weather's humid. Knicks lost. What do you do?

SELENA: I sell make-up.

JONATHAN: Great. Why are you in such a bad mood?

SELENA: I'm in a bad...because...it's none of your business.

JONATHAN: That doesn't mean you shouldn't tell me. Maybe talking about it'll make you feel better.

SELENA: With a total stranger?

JONATHAN: O K. Hi, I'm Jonathan Kaplan. I graduated from Yale two years ago with a degree in English lit A K A "you want fries with that". That's a joke. Sorry. My Father is an analyst. Not of people but of numbers. Don't ask, I don't know what it means either. My Mother's a Jewish Mother. Nuff said. Despite the statistics, they're still happily married. I grew up on Long Island and am very happy to be living in the city though I wish I had more money because then I

fantasize that I might actually enjoy myself. On the
other hand, I desperately want to live in the country
because then I fantasize I might actually enjoy myself.
I spend a disproportionate amount of time convincing
myself that I can live both in the City and in the country
at the same time. When not actively engaged in self-
delusion, I spend my time writing a novel but then,
who doesn't? Or at least who didn't until writing the
great American software code took over for writing
the great American novel. I'm not terribly athletic but
I religiously read the sports page and get angrier when
the Knicks miss a foul shot than I do when the U S
bombs a foreign country. I have an older brother,
Marty, who went to M I T, partnered up with some
friends in Seattle on "Here's something you don't
need"-dot-com and made a buzzillion dollars. Then
lost a buzziliion dollars. He has stopped returning my
phone calls. I have a younger sister, Jessica, who insists
that everyone call her Selena because she feels the pain
of the murdered Latin American rock star, and who just
dropped out of school for the second time. This time to
follow her forty-five year old ex-hippie boyfriend on
a trek through the Himalayas. She doesn't believe in
phones despite the obvious evidence to the contrary.
I imagine that one day I'll recount this time in my life to
my wife or my kids or my mistress I suppose if things
go terribly wrong, and I'll reminisce about how great
it was and how happy I felt, but right now, I gotta tell
you, it feels like crap. I definitely aspire to greatness
but eagerly accept mediocrity. I try to think globally
and act locally, but mostly I just eat a lot of Haagen-
Dazs. I prefer Autumn to spring, feel stupid in shorts,
and look forward to one day actually needing a suit for
something other than a funeral or wedding. I consider
myself a "cautious realist" while most people consider
me a raging pessimist. And although I don't believe in
God, and have nothing resembling faith in the spiritual,

yesterday I went to a fucking palm reader because if I don't make some human contact soon, I'm going to shoot myself. Now then, I have about seven minutes, why the fuck are you in such a bad mood?

SELENA: My name's Selena too.

JONATHAN: What?

SELENA: Like your sister.

JONATHAN: Her name is Jessica. Do you believe in soulmates?

SELENA: Soulmates? No.

JONATHAN: Well, I don't know, maybe we'd just... compliment each other well. I mean, it can't hurt to talk for ten minutes and find out.

(She is taken in by this, then stops herself.)

SELENA: You know what? You've all got your bullshit but as soon as things get tough, you're history.

JONATHAN: I'm not....

SELENA: Look, you're a nice guy O K? A little desperate maybe and probably in need of some psychological counseling, but basically nice. Maybe in another time, in another place we could hang out. But I gotta go.

JONATHAN: Please don't leave.

SELENA: It was a thrill meeting you.

JONATHAN: Just talk to me.

SELENA: Good luck with your novel. *(She is leaving.)*

JONATHAN: What did you say? Oh my God.

(She is gone. Beat. JONATHAN looks at the BARTENDER.)

JONATHAN: Can I have another beer?

BARTENDER: You didn't drink your first one. Jonathan drinks the beer in one gulp.

JONATHAN: Can I have another beer?

(BARTENDER *gets the beer.*)

BARTENDER: You come on a little strong, don't you?

JONATHAN: You're critiquing me?

BARTENDER: Sorry. Hey, I believe in a soul mate.

JONATHAN: You do?

BARTENDER: Yup.

JONATHAN: What is it?

BARTENDER: I'll tell you what it's not. It's not finding someone exactly like you. Same interests, same way of dealing with the world, all that nonsense. It's just finding someone who makes you better.

JONATHAN: That's all I was trying to say.

BARTENDER: Just cause she didn't hear it doesn't make it not so.

JONATHAN: Barstool philosophy.

BARTENDER: That's the best kind when you're sitting on a barstool. So uh, a guy's gotta ask: what happens at midnight?

JONATHAN: One of two things. I either go home and kill myself...or I don't.

BARTENDER: So the same thing that happens every midnight.

JONATHAN: More or less.

BARTENDER: So what makes this night different from all other nights?

JONATHAN: Well, rabbi...

BARTENDER: Yes?

JONATHAN: Tonight I really believed I'd find her.

BARTENDER: Your soul mate?

JONATHAN: Yup. No more bashfully staring at girls in the park, no more going to parties and not talking to anyone, no more sitting at home, feeling like I'd do better with a blow-up doll, pining for the past. Tonight I actually put it all on the line, and look what happens.

BARTENDER: Well maybe that was her.

JONATHAN: Yeah?

BARTENDER: She said, maybe in another time, another place, timing's everything you know.

JONATHAN: Whatever.

BARTENDER: Maybe it just wasn't meant to happen tonight. Maybe Tuesday's are bad for soul mate catching. Hey...maybe I'm your soul mate.

JONATHAN: I don't think so.

BARTENDER: Why not? You think your soul mate can only come wrapped up in some tight little mini-skirt? I like Haagen Dazs too.

JONATHAN: You're not quite what I had in mind.

BARTENDER: That doesn't make it not so.

JONATHAN: You're my soul mate?

BARTENDER: It's possible.

JONATHAN: How would I know?

BARTENDER: You want to try an experiment?

JONATHAN: An experiment?

BARTENDER: Won't hurt. Very simple. Like a test. See if we're on the same wavelength.

JONATHAN: Sure.

(BARTENDER *takes out a deck of cards from behind the bar.*)

JONATHAN: You're gonna do a card trick?

BARTENDER: It's not a trick, it's a test. It's a new deck. Break the seal.

(BARTENDER *hands the deck to* JONATHAN *who opens it and gives it back.*)

BARTENDER: I'll leave the Jokers in. *(He starts shuffling the deck.)*

JONATHAN: I don't believe in tricks.

BARTENDER: It's not a trick. It's just a test. It's no big deal. O K. shuffled? *(He hands the deck to* JONATHAN.*)* Cut 'em.

(JONATHAN *does.* BARTENDER *spreads the cards out face down on the bar.*)

BARTENDER: Alright. I'm gonna turn around. You pull out any card you want and look at it O K?

(BARTENDER *turns his back.* JONATHAN *takes a card, looks at it.*

JONATHAN: O K.

BARTENDER: O K. Now there's no way I could know what that card is, is there?

JONATHAN: No.

BARTENDER: Good. Concentrate. Think about the card. See it in your head. Send a vision of it out to your soul mate. Say the name of the card over and over in your mind like you were telling someone your deepest secret. *(He turns around and looks* JONATHAN *deep in the eye.)* Seven of clubs.

JONATHAN: Holy shit.

(BARTENDER *starts collecting the cards.*)

JONATHAN: How? That's not possible.

BARTENDER: I just saw it in my head.

JONATHAN: How did you do that?

BARTENDER: I don't know. It's just a soul mate thing.

JONATHAN: Maybe you are my soul mate.

BARTENDER: Maybe so.

JONATHAN: My name's Jonathan.

BARTENDER: Nice to meet you.

(They look into each other's eyes.)

BARTENDER: Look you're a nice guy. I'm gonna do you a favor.

*(*BARTENDER *holds up the cards, spreads them out on the bar, face up.* JONATHAN *looks at them.)*

JONATHAN: They're all the seven of clubs.

BARTENDER: You know how many guys I've gone home with? Trick costs two ninety five. Cheapest guaranteed lay in town.

JONATHAN: Why did you show me that?

BARTENDER: Because you told me your name. And I saw how easy it would be to take you home and fuck you. And I saw you actually having a good time despite yourself. But then I wouldn't call you. And you'd sit by the phone and cry. Well, I'm gonna close the bar now. It's midnight and the place is empty. But I just want to say one thing. You wanna find your soul mate? That's great. Just do yourself a favor. Be patient, and do the work O K? Quit looking for tricks.

JONATHAN: I'm an asshole.

BARTENDER: No. You're a kid.

*(*JONATHAN *stands.)*

BARTENDER: Hey, did you say your parents were still happily married despite the statistics?

JONATHAN: Yeah.

BARTENDER: Then why don't you go call them and tell them you love them?

(JONATHAN *reaches for his wallet.*)

JONATHAN: What do I owe you?

BARTENDER: On me.

(JONATHAN *heads for the exit.*)

BARTENDER: Hey, Jonathan?

JONATHAN: Yeah?

BARTENDER: What's it gonna be?

JONATHAN: What's what going to be?

BARTENDER: You gonna go home and kill yourself?

JONATHAN: I don't know. I'll tell you tomorrow.

(JONATHAN *exits.* BARTENDER *starts closing up. The lights start to fade.* BARTENDER *practices his joke to himself.*)

BARTENDER: Guys walks into a bar with an octopus, says to the bartender, I'll bet you a hundred dollars this octopus can play any musical instrument in this bar.

(SELENA *runs in, out of breath much as* JONATHAN *had. She scares the* BARTENDER.)

SELENA: Did he leave?

BARTENDER: Wh...? Oh. Yeah.

(*This hits her hard as...*)

(*Lights fade to black.*)

Scene Five
A started stopped watch

(The FORTUNE TELLER *is an exotic older woman from Eastern Europe.)*

(The mysterious parlor room of the FORTUNE TELLER.*)*

(A title slide, placard, banner or something: MONDAY (The day before))

(The FORTUNE TELLER *sits at a table. At length she speaks.)*

FORTUNE TELLER: Come in.

*(*JONATHAN *enters. He looks nervous and haggard.)*

JONATHAN: Hello.

FORTUNE TELLER: Sit down.

JONATHAN: I...

FORTUNE TELLER: I don't bite.

JONATHAN: I'm here to...

FORTUNE TELLER: Have your fortune told. Yes. That's why one comes to a fortune teller.

JONATHAN: Do you...?

FORTUNE TELLER: Tell the truth?

JONATHAN: Tell fortunes.

FORTUNE TELLER: It's the same. Sit down. Please.

JONATHAN: How much will it cost?

FORTUNE TELLER: It depends.

JONATHAN: I've never done this before.

FORTUNE TELLER: Relax. I'm not a prostitute. But I
suppose my services are comparable. You pay me.
I give you something you want.

JONATHAN: What's that?

FORTUNE TELLER: I said: the truth.

JONATHAN: So how much?

FORTUNE TELLER: What's your pleasure? Tea leaves?
Tarot cards? Read your palm?

JONATHAN: What's the difference?

FORTUNE TELLER: The difference doesn't matter—
your fortune is the same.

JONATHAN: So then...?

FORTUNE TELLER: I'll read your palm.

JONATHAN: How will I know it's the truth?

FORTUNE TELLER: You'll know when the things I say
will happen—happen.

JONATHAN: Guaranteed?

FORTUNE TELLER: Guaranteed.

JONATHAN: How much?

FORTUNE TELLER: Ten dollars. What do you lose?
Jonathan takes out his wallet and gives her ten dollars.

FORTUNE TELLER: Give me your hands.

(He does. She holds his hand palm up and runs her
fingers over his palm almost sexually. He leans in,
interested.)

FORTUNE TELLER: You have beautiful hands. This is
your life line. You see this here? This interruption. You
will have a near death experience. A car crash perhaps.
This line represents wealth. It intersects early and
breaks away. You will inherit money. Or make it. Then

lose it. Gambling maybe. Or a deal gone bad. I'm sorry.
You will never have the wealth you'll have in youth.
Maybe that's not just money.

JONATHAN: You're kind of a mean fortune teller.

FORTUNE TELLER: You want a nice fortune? Read your
horoscope. Open a fortune cookie. You come to me,
you get the truth. You get what you need. It's not my
fault you have a sad life Jonathan.

JONATHAN: My name.

FORTUNE TELLER: What?

JONATHAN: I didn't tell you my name.

FORTUNE TELLER: Is it Jonathan?

JONATHAN: Yes.

FORTUNE TELLER: So relax. Alright. We did life. We did
wealth. There's only one more people care about.

JONATHAN: Love.

FORTUNE TELLER: Yes.

JONATHAN: And?

FORTUNE TELLER: This is your love line. You see how
it's cut into your hand. Deep but faraway.

JONATHAN: What does that mean?

FORTUNE TELLER: It's unclear. With age it will become
deeper, or it will fade away. One of the extremes.
What will determine this Jonathan?

JONATHAN: What? I don't know.

FORTUNE TELLER: Perhaps you're not ready to...

JONATHAN: I am. I want to.

FORTUNE TELLER: What is this? *(She's pointing to his
hand.)* Tell me. A deep mark on the lifeline. A pain.
A sharp pain. Tell me Jonathan of this pain.

JONATHAN: I don't know.

FORTUNE TELLER: I can't help you if you won't help me.
A death perhaps. Did someone close to you die?

(JONATHAN *is holding back tears.*)

FORTUNE TELLER: It's alright. I'm feeling a K. Kristen?
Karen?

JONATHAN: Kara.

FORTUNE TELLER: Would you like to speak to her?

JONATHAN: What?

FORTUNE TELLER: Through me. I'm a medium.
To the dead. A portal. If you wish.

JONATHAN: You can speak to Kara?

FORTUNE TELLER: I can channel her.

JONATHAN: I don't understand.

FORTUNE TELLER: She will speak through me. You will
feel her presence. You can speak to her channeled
through me but only for a very short time.

JONATHAN: Alright.

FORTUNE TELLER: You'd like to?

JONATHAN: Yes.

FORTUNE TELLER: But this is more. Expensive. The cost.
It's extra. A medium, not a fortune teller. If you still
want to...

JONATHAN: Yes. Alright. How much?

FORTUNE TELLER: A hundred dollars.

JONATHAN: A hundred? The palm was only ten.

FORTUNE TELLER: The future is easy. The dead...
that's difficult. Very taxing. On me. You don't have to,
if you don't want...

JONATHAN: No, alright. If I can be sure it's really her.

FORTUNE TELLER: I'll tell you what. Because I like you, if you don't think it's her, if you don't think it's true, I'll give you your money back alright?

JONATHAN: O K. *(He takes a hundred dollars out of his wallet and gives it to her.)*

FORTUNE TELLER: Our special Monday money back guarantee. Good. You don't have anything of hers do you? A physical possession she once owned? That would make channeling her easier. Faster.

JONATHAN: I do. *(He takes a small pocket watch out of his pocket and gives it to her.)*

FORTUNE TELLER: A watch. Very beautiful. Old.

JONATHAN: It was her Grandfather's. She wore it around her neck. I took it. Right off the body. I just...wanted it. I thought she'd want me to.

FORTUNE TELLER: I'm sure she did. It doesn't work.

JONATHAN: It does. I just stopped it. To freeze the time when she... it just needs a winding.

FORTUNE TELLER: Alright. Let's start. Relax. Take a deep breath. Take my hands. Look me in the eye and whatever you do, do not break eye contact with me. Do you understand?

JONATHAN: Yes.

FORTUNE TELLER: This is very important.

JONATHAN: O K.

FORTUNE TELLER: Alright.

(They hold hands across the table. The FORTUNE TELLER *rocks slowly back and forth. The lights change. Perhaps underscoring. An energy seems to pass between* JONATHAN

and the FORTUNE TELLER. *For him it is like being filled with the warmth of love, for her it is like an electrical current.)*

FORTUNE TELLER: She's here.

JONATHAN: Kara?

FORTUNE TELLER: It is her.

JONATHAN: How can I be sure?

FORTUNE TELLER: Think of something. A time. A time only she would know. And she'll tell me. Are you thinking? Think harder. Concentrate. Yes. A happy time. You and her. Together. Out doors. Walking. The sun. And both of you in love. You were younger then. Not just in age but...

JONATHAN: I've missed you so much.

FORTUNE TELLER: She knows. She's alright. She wants you to know that she's alright.

JONATHAN: Why did you do it?

FORTUNE TELLER: She says she felt she had to.

JONATHAN: No note. Nothing. Finding you like that.

FORTUNE TELLER: She says she's sorry. She never wanted to hurt you. She says she didn't know how to say goodbye. How could she? To you? How could she?

JONATHAN: I miss you.

(The FORTUNE TELLER *speaks in a younger voice without an accent.)*

FORTUNE TELLER: I know. I feel your thoughts. I'm dead but I'm not gone. I don't regret what I did, Jonathan, I don't.

JONATHAN: Oh Kara, please tell me why.

(The FORTUNE TELLER *grabs his face and keeps his attention locked on her.)*

FORTUNE TELLER: Why doesn't matter. It's time for you to move on.

JONATHAN: I can't, I need to know, I've tried.

FORTUNE TELLER: Not as hard as you must. It's what I want. It's what you want. It's ok to open your heart. Surrender again. Move forward. Let go.

JONATHAN: I'm scared.

FORTUNE TELLER: You should be scared. And that's O K.

JONATHAN: I want to see you.

FORTUNE TELLER: There's nothing to see anymore.

(JONATHAN, *overcome, breaks eye contact. The* FORTUNE TELLER *releases* JONATHAN *as her voice returns.*)

FORTUNE TELLER: She's leaving.

JONATHAN: No wait, please. Stay and talk with me. I can't believe I'm actually...with you again. Talk with me.

FORTUNE TELLER: She cannot.

JONATHAN: Please.

FORTUNE TELLER: She says she's sorry. (*Young voice*) Good luck with your novel. Good bye. (*Older voice*) She's gone.

(*The lights slowly return.*)

FORTUNE TELLER: How did it go? Do I owe you a hundred dollars?

JONATHAN: Oh God.

FORTUNE TELLER: Did she help?

JONATHAN: Yes.

FORTUNE TELLER: I'm sorry Jonathan. Are we finished?

JONATHAN: I guess so.

FORTUNE TELLER: But... What? You want something else yes?

JONATHAN: Yes.

FORTUNE TELLER: Love. You want love.

JONATHAN: Yes.

FORTUNE TELLER: Alright. I can help you more.

JONATHAN: How?

FORTUNE TELLER: It's your soul mate you lost. I feel in you that loss deeply. But we have others. There's more than one. I can help you fill your wish. To find. Again. To love.

JONATHAN: What do I do?

FORTUNE TELLER: But it's more.

JONATHAN: What?

FORTUNE TELLER: The cost. A fortune teller has to make a living. It's more.

JONATHAN: How much.

FORTUNE TELLER: One hundred more.

JONATHAN: This gets expensive very quickly.

FORTUNE TELLER: You get what you pay for.

JONATHAN: You take credit cards?

FORTUNE TELLER: Cash.

JONATHAN: I don't have it.

FORTUNE TELLER: It's up to you.

(Pause)

JONATHAN: What about the watch?

FORTUNE TELLER: The watch?

JONATHAN: I'll give it to you. It's an antique. It's gotta be worth...

(*She picks it up. Looks it over*)

FORTUNE TELLER: I don't know.

JONATHAN: It's a great deal. Worth at least a hundred.

FORTUNE TELLER: I can't take your...what would I do with a watch?

JONATHAN: Tell the time.

FORTUNE TELLER: I know the time, I'm a fortune teller. (*She hands him the watch.*)

JONATHAN: Sell it. Give it as a gift. No, wait, look, it's moving again.

FORTUNE TELLER: So it is. Are you sure you want to give this up?

(*He nods yes.*)

FORTUNE TELLER: Well, if it will help. Alright.

JONATHAN: Thank you.

(*The* FORTUNE TELLER *takes the watch and smiles.*)

FORTUNE TELLER: We will write your wish in the book of life....

JONATHAN: And I can wish for anything? I can wish to meet my soul mate tomorrow?

FORTUNE TELLER: You can also wish for something inside.

JONATHAN: No. That's what I want. And it's guaranteed to come true?

FORTUNE TELLER: ...

JONATHAN: Please?

FORTUNE TELLER: Alright. Yes. It is guaranteed.

JONATHAN: Really?

FORTUNE TELLER: Sure. One hundred percent. Guaranteed.

(Lights fade to black.)

Scene Six
The Grand Canyon blinks

(A hotel room. A bed. A mirror)

(A title slide, placard, banner or something: SUNDAY (The day before))

(SELENA stands holding an open Tiffany ring box. WEINSTEIN looks on. She closes the box.)

SELENA: I can't.

WEINSTEIN: Selena...

SELENA: I'm sorry.

WEINSTEIN: You said you'd think about it.

SELENA: I did. A lot. I'm sorry, I just can't marry you right now.

WEINSTEIN: Can you tell me why?

SELENA: You know why.

WEINSTEIN: I don't know why.

SELENA: You know, the first time we met, here in this room, I knew things wouldn't go right for us but I had the reasons wrong.

WEINSTEIN: What were the reasons?

SELENA: I thought you would dump me.

WEINSTEIN: How could I? ever?

SELENA: You could. You could have. I thought you could have.

WEINSTEIN: You didn't know me then.

SELENA: No.

WEINSTEIN: So what are the reasons now?

SELENA: It's just...not what I want my life to be. Someone's trophy.

WEINSTEIN: You're not my....

SELENA: I'm half your age.

WEINSTEIN: Well my age isn't exactly news. That hasn't stood in our way so far.

SELENA: Look, it's not ultimately what you want either. I'm not what you need.

WEINSTEIN: Please don't tell me what I want. If you can't handle your own happiness, that's no reason to take it out on me.

SELENA: You want something easy.

WEINSTEIN: I'm not looking for something easy. It takes work, I know that.

SELENA: You haven't shown me that.

WEINSTEIN: What?

SELENA: Prove it.

WEINSTEIN: How? It's not something that can be proved.

SELENA: You can try....

WEINSTEIN: I'm not a knight in shining....

SELENA: You still wear your wife's ring for God's sake, you idolize her, like she was perfect. She wasn't perfect. Every story you tell about her is...

WEINSTEIN: What does that have to do with you?

SELENA: What does it...?

WEINSTEIN: It's totally different.

SELENA: What!?

(Pause)

WEINSTEIN: Well I have to say I'm not surprised. I'm disappointed, but not surprised. I guess I sort of knew it all along, something like it, from the first night we met.

(The lights change abruptly. SELENA and WEINSTEIN change their attitudes. It is a flashback. Suddenly, they are kissing passionately. SELENA has WEINSTEIN up against a wall or the bed post or something. He is moaning. She is rubbing her body into him.)

SELENA: Mmm.

WEINSTEIN: Oh, Oh God.

(She puts her hand on his crotch.)

WEINSTEIN: Oh. Oh my...that's...wait...let me get a....

SELENA: Unzip. *(She puts her hand inside his pants.)*

WEINSTEIN: Wait. Just a minute. Hold on.

(She continues to rub.)

WEINSTEIN: Oh my God.

SELENA: Mmm. Come on baby.

WEINSTEIN: Hold on, wait. Oh God, Oh my God.

(He ejaculates in his pants. He shudders while she holds him.)

WEINSTEIN: Oh my God. I'm sorry.

SELENA: That's alright.

WEINSTEIN: Wow. Oh.

SELENA: Let me get you a towel. *(She exits.)*

WEINSTEIN: I didn't mean to....

SELENA: *(O S)* It's O K, we'll do it again.

WEINSTEIN: I haven't done that since high school.

SELENA: *(O S)* It's alright.

WEINSTEIN: It's just that it's been so long. It felt so good.

(SELENA re-enters.)

SELENA: Clean yourself up.

(She gives him the towel. He exits into the bathroom, walking awkwardly. SELENA goes to a mirror. Reapplies her lipstick, puts her hair up again, straightens out her clothes.)

WEINSTEIN: *(O S)* You still there?

SELENA: Don't worry. I'm not going anywhere.

(WEINSTEIN re-enters.)

WEINSTEIN: I'm sorry, I don't usually....

SELENA: Please. I'm flattered.

WEINSTEIN: It just, it makes me feel....

SELENA: Yes?

WEINSTEIN: Young. I'm a little dizzy. I should lie down.

(SELENA leads him to the bed. He lies down.)

SELENA: It's alright. You sleep. I'll take care of you.
Sleep. Rest. Dream.

(He lays down and falls asleep. She strokes his hair.)

SELENA: As soon as we laid eyes on each other it was
like we knew. Sitting at the bar. We caught eyes. What
a feeling of...power. If every moment could be like that,
then life would be...magic. The future wouldn't be scary
it would be...right. But the future is so...vast. The Grand
Canyon blinks and we are dust. So if the moment can't

stretch forever, then how do you make it last? Me?
I'll reach for the stars, but settle for what I get. I'll enjoy
the now. I'll hide behind my make-up, show you only
what you want to see. But eventually you'll tire of me.
I'll cry but the world will keep turning. Ah, I'm
babbling. You sleep, and I'll sleep too. I'll sleep and
wonder what you're dreaming. Wonder what you
were dreaming the night that we first met.

(She lays down to sleep. WEINSTEIN *sits up. The lights
change. We are now in a dream inside a flashback.)*

WEINSTEIN: I'm dreaming. Tired, comfortable, I'm
dreaming I'm a soldier. I'm in some sort of army
hospital. My face is burned. A layered, covered mess
of bandage. There is a young, alluring nurse who tends
to me. She washes clean my bandages and soothes my
burns. Through my new face of gauze I barely make her
out. Like I'm in some bad remake of the English Patient
or something. She speaks to me, some babble of the
future. Two doctors come and argue over me. It's Stern
and Kaplan.

*(*STERN *and* KAPLAN *enter dressed as doctors.)*

WEINSTEIN: They look beneath my bandages and see
my face. They look confused, disturbed, they look
revolted. They strap me to the bed so when I see myself,
I cannot harm myself. Finally Kaplan says:

KAPLAN: Have you guys seen those new Sony laptops?
What's his name upstairs has one. Fucking light as a
feather.

*(*STERN *and* KAPLAN *exit.)*

WEINSTEIN: My heart begins to pound. My blood is
rushing to my face. My face so hot on fire. Nurse!
Where's my nurse to cool my burning face? To make
me feel alright, alive. I need her like I need the air to
breathe, to live, to love. Again. I want to break out free.

To tear these bandages from off my face, but I am
strapped down to the bed, as helpless as a child. Finally
she comes and starts to unwrap all the gauze. I fear my
head will disappear: like the invisible man. Without the
gauze, without the pain, I fear that I might cease to be.
I scream that "I'm not ready!, I'm not ready!" But she
undoes the gauze like skin from off an onion. My blood
is pounding harder, faster. The final strips of gauze
collect and wrap around her hands like a cat's cradle.
She sees my face and screams! I turn to see the nurse
but she's become my wife. She holds a scalpel tightly
in her hand. She slashes at my face. I want to stop her,
do... something, anything, but I am strapped down to
the bed. She flays my skin from off my face, the scalpel
hot as fire, slashing, cutting til I am reduced to nothing
more than just a bloody oozing skeleton.

(The lights change back and SELENA *and* WEINSTEIN *resume
their positions from before the flashback.)*

WEINSTEIN: Well, I have to say I'm not surprised.
Disappointed. Not surprised. I guess I sort of knew it
all along, something like it, from the first night we met.

SELENA: So what does this mean for us?

WEINSTEIN: I guess it means we're over.

SELENA: You don't want to still...?

WEINSTEIN: Do you? What's the point?

SELENA: You can't freeze time can you? A feeling in
time. Do you know that yesterday at the counter I sold
this woman a new shade of lipstick? Typical woman
I get- rich bitch. Not afraid of anything. So for twenty
years or something she's worn the same lipstick and
one day she decides to change. I asked her why all of
a sudden? She said "maybe my husband will notice
me again". It's not about lipstick is it?

WEINSTEIN: No. No it's not. You were a fantasy for me. Too good to be true. Back to real life I suppose. And you? You'll find someone your own age. He'll tell you his life story and if the connection is right, you'll make him the happiest man in the world.

SELENA: And you'll find someone, not your wife, but someone better.

WEINSTEIN: Maybe.

SELENA: You will.

WEINSTEIN: Maybe.

SELENA: Still friends?

WEINSTEIN: Friends? No. But I'll think of you. I'll think of you all the time. *(He heads for the door.)*

SELENA: John?

(SELENA holds the box out for him to take. He doesn't take it.)

(He looks at her and goes to exit again.)

SELENA: John?

(He stops and looks at her.)

SELENA: If you had fought for me, I might have said yes.

(Lights go to black.)

Scene Seven
Taken to the gate

(At the gate of an airport.)

(A title slide, placard, banner or something: SATURDAY (The day before))

(SHEILA and MR GOLDBERG sit next to each other passing time. She is reading a magazine, he is drinking a coffee. Her expensive carry on luggage sits nearby. They stay like this for

a long time, not speaking. He absent mindedly sipping coffee,
she looking at pictures and turning pages. After awhile,
he spills coffee on his suit.)

MR GOLDBERG: Ah, shit.

SHEILA: What now?

MR GOLDBERG: Nothing. Coffee.

SHEILA: On your...oh for God's sake.

MR GOLDBERG: It's nothing, I got it.

SHEILA: Here, let me...

MR GOLDBERG: I got it, I got it, it's fine.

SHEILA: Go to the bathroom and...

MR GOLDBERG: I said I got it. No big deal.

SHEILA: Consuela can get it out. That woman's a
Goddess. Is there anything she can't do?

MR GOLDBERG: Uh-huh.

SHEILA: Without her you'd be completely at a loss.
(She goes back to reading. Abruptly stops) You don't have
to stay here you know.

MR GOLDBERG: What, I'm waiting with you.

SHEILA: I'm a big girl, I know how to board a plane.

MR GOLDBERG: I thought it would be nice to keep you
company. Like I always do it.

SHEILA: Well do you want to talk about something?

MR GOLDBERG: Like what?

SHEILA: I don't know. But if I'm just going to sit here
and read my magazine, I can just as well do it by
myself. If you want to keep me company, keep me
company.

MR GOLDBERG: Alright.

SHEILA: Alright what?

MR GOLDBERG: Alright, I'll keep you company.

(She puts the magazine down. Beat)

SHEILA: Well what do you want to talk about?

MR GOLDBERG: I don't know.

SHEILA: Well, this is riveting.

MR GOLDBERG: Well what do you want to talk about?

SHEILA: You don't like to talk about the things that I like to talk about.

MR GOLDBERG: Sheila...

SHEILA: Which is fine. I learned this a long time ago. It's fine. We don't have to talk about those things.

MR GOLDBERG: What don't I like to talk about?

SHEILA: I don't want to have this fight with you right before I get on a plane.

MR GOLDBERG: Just tell me.

SHEILA: What time is it?

MR GOLDBERG: Tell me.

SHEILA: The garden.

MR GOLDBERG: Oh please.

SHEILA: What?

MR GOLDBERG: The garden?

SHEILA: You don't like to...

MR GOLDBERG: What else?

SHEILA: My friends.

MR GOLDBERG: Your...?

SHEILA: You don't care.

MR GOLDBERG: About your friends?

SHEILA: You don't. Your friends, yes. Not mine.

MR GOLDBERG: I thought they were our friends.

SHEILA: Please.

MR GOLDBERG: Anything else?

SHEILA: What bothers you. You never talk about what bothers you.

MR GOLDBERG: Like what?

SHEILA: I don't know. I don't know what bothers you, you won't talk about it.

MR GOLDBERG: Nothing bothers me.

SHEILA: Nothing bothers you? Life is perfect. You have no complaints.

MR GOLDBERG: Not really. No.

SHEILA: Fine, then I guess there's nothing to talk about.

(Pause)

MR GOLDBERG: So we can only talk about things that bother us? We can only complain? That's the only thing to talk about?

SHEILA: Can you please stop, you're being ridiculous and you're giving me a headache.

MR GOLDBERG: How am I being ridiculous?

SHEILA: Please!?

MR GOLDBERG: Tell me how.

SHEILA: You don't think what you're saying is ridiculous?

MR GOLDBERG: No.

SHEILA: Fine.

MR GOLDBERG: Good.

SHEILA: Fine.

(Pause)

MR GOLDBERG: Alright, you want to know something that's bothering me? I'm thinking about quitting my job, how 'bout that?

SHEILA: What? Why would you quit your job?

MR GOLDBERG: Because I am a powerless underling who spends my days feeling like shit and who is continually asked to do things I don't agree with like manipulate facts.

SHEILA: That's ridiculous.

MR GOLDBERG: I'm serious.

SHEILA: You have a family! You have responsibilities. Y...You're a grown up. You can't just throw something good away in order to have more fun.

MR GOLDBERG: I can't?

SHEILA: Absolutely not. I forbid it.

MR GOLDBERG: I knew that's what you'd say.

(Pause)

SHEILA: Don't do it. Don't you dare do it.

?(Pause)

MR GOLDBERG: Sheila, why are we still married?

SHEILA: What?

MR GOLDBERG: I mean, do we still love each other? I drove you out to the airport, paid sixteen hundred and four dollars for a ticket I have no intention of using just so I could sit with you at the gate. I thought that was a very nice thing to do. I have plenty of other things I could be doing. We don't see each other much.

And all we do is bicker like two old cows. What is that? What is wrong with us?

SHEILA: Cows don't bicker.

MR GOLDBERG: What?

SHEILA: In what ways do cows bicker? How are we like bickering cows?

MR GOLDBERG: Is that what you heard in what I just said?

SHEILA: I just think you should choose your words more carefully. You have a large vocabulary, use it. Express yourself properly. No wonder Daniel's failing English. Do you know that he doesn't even know what a preposition is?

MR GOLDBERG: Right. You're right. Sorry.

(Pause)

SHEILA: But to answer your question: I think we love each other very much. We may not show it all the time. We may have our routines, some unpleasant routines, but that's certainly no reason to question our marriage. We married each other because we were equals and we are still equals. We're married, and we'll stay married.

MR GOLDBERG: Simple as that?

(SHEILA *looks him dead in the eye.*)

SHEILA: We'll do the things we need to do to keep ourselves married. And we'll *both* find what we need to find where we need to find it. Is that clear?

(Pause)

MR GOLDBERG: Clear.

SHEILA: Good. *(Pause)* Oh, by the way, remind Consuela, Izzy's coming tomorrow.

MR GOLDBERG: Who's Izzy?

SHEILA: Izzy, you know, that funny electrical man.

MR GOLDBERG: I thought he came yesterday.

SHEILA: He did. But he couldn't fit a something with
the thing he...I don't know, what am I some sort of
electrical expert all of a sudden!? The point is he's
coming back tomorrow.

MR GOLDBERG: Sorry. O K. Izzy tomorrow. *(Pause)*
Tomorrow's Sunday.

SHEILA: He's coming back tomorrow because I need
him back! I need him back, so he's coming back! If I say
I need him Sunday, then Goddamn it, he will go out of
his way to give me what I need! I asked you could you
please remind Consuela. Why is this so Goddamn
difficult?

MR GOLDBERG: Fine. O K. He's coming Sunday.

(Pause)

SHEILA: What would you do if I told you to stop?

MR GOLDBERG: Are you?

SHEILA: I'm asking a question.

MR GOLDBERG: I'd stop.

SHEILA: Fine then. *(Pause)* So what do you think of my
lipstick?

MR GOLDBERG: What?

SHEILA: It's new. It's different. You didn't even notice.
Do you like it?

MR GOLDBERG: Sure. It's fine.

SHEILA: "Fine"?

MR GOLDBERG: Nice. It's good.

SHEILA: Yeah?

MR GOLDBERG: Yeah.

SHEILA: So you like it?

MR GOLDBERG: You look beautiful.

SHEILA: Thank you. Was that so hard to say?

(Pause)

VOICE: Ladies and gentlemen this is the preboarding call for flight eight twenty two to Seattle, all first class passengers, and passengers needing assistance or with small children may now board the aircraft.

SHEILA: Well, that's me.

MR GOLDBERG: Hang on. Stay another minute. You don't have to get on just yet.

SHEILA: Might as well.

MR GOLDBERG: Wait. Remember that summer, that first summer after we met, that you spent backpacking around France?

SHEILA: Yes?

MR GOLDBERG: I think I cried all summer. Like a little schoolchild.

SHEILA: So?

MR GOLDBERG: And you wrote to me. You wrote me every single day. And I guess I've taken you to the gate ever since.

SHEILA: And I appreciate it.

MR GOLDBERG: But you don't write me every day anymore.

SHEILA: Well that would be a bit excessive don't you think.

MR GOLDBERG: You don't even call.

SHEILA: You're never home. God forbid I disturb you at work.

MR GOLDBERG: Do you know that when Linda McCartney died they said that she and Paul had spent every night of their marriage together except for six nights or something when he was in jail for marijuana.

SHEILA: You're comparing our marriage to the life of a rock star?

MR GOLDBERG: I'm just wondering.

SHEILA: What?

MR GOLDBERG: What happens? What happened?

SHEILA: We're not rock stars O K? And we're not in a fairy-tale. What we have is twenty years of...history. And that means something. Don't rock the boat now O K? It's too late. It's insulting. You had your chance. We have a good marriage. Compared to most of the people we know we have a great marriage. Nothing's perfect. Leave it at that.

MR GOLDBERG: Right. Sorry. *(Pause)* She collects her bags and starts to head off.

SHEILA: Well. I'll be back before you notice I was gone.

MR GOLDBERG: O K.

SHEILA: Make sure Izzy does a good job.

MR GOLDBERG: I will.

SHEILA: And don't let Consuela mess anything up while I'm gone.

MR GOLDBERG: I won't.

(She looks at him.)

MR GOLDBERG: Trust me. I won't. Lights fade to black.

Scene Eight
Something for the house

(A bar)

(Title slide, placard, banner or something: FRIDAY (one week ago today))

(IZZY sits at the bar drinking a beer. Another full beer sits on the bar next to him. After a long moment FRANK enters with a large, plain white shopping bag.)

FRANK: Jesus, Izzy I'm sorry I'm so late.

IZZY: No problem.

FRANK: Fucking traffic.

IZZY: No big deal Frank, don't worry about it.

FRANK: If you took all the time you were late in your life, all that time spent just being, what, late, and you, you know, added it up, you would have days, whole days back for yourself to do whatever you want.

IZZY: Yeah, right. Here, I ordered you a beer. You want it?

FRANK: Of course I want it. What am I suddenly gonna start drinking tequila sunrises or something? *(He sips the beer.)* So. What's going on?

IZZY: Nothing.

FRANK: No?

IZZY: You know. You?

FRANK: Same shit different day.

IZZY: Yeah.

FRANK: You coming over Sunday watch the game?

IZZY: Course.

FRANK: Good. Mack coming?

IZZY: Course.

FRANK: Good. You're not bringing Cathy though right?, no women.

IZZY: No.

FRANK: Good.

IZZY: Oh but hey, I might be late though. Get this. I'm installing this lighting system for these Park Avenue yahoos right? They have switches, only they don't want switches, they want dimmers now right? Set the mood for parties better or whatever. So I'm installing the dimmers talking to this crazy lady. Probably sits at home all day while her husband's out making money, lonely, nobody to talk to, you know the type.

FRANK: Sure.

IZZY: So, she wants to know if these dimmers are the best. So I tell her about these other kinds of dimmers that just turn on the light with a touch of your finger. High end stuff right? I'm already halfway through the job, and she goes apeshit. This she has to have. So it's stop everything, hold the horses. Can't you do it today? Anyway, long story short, I'm going back Sunday to put in a whole new system.

FRANK: You're going in on a Sunday?

IZZY: You kidding? I love it. Charge her twice as much money.

FRANK: Yeah?

IZZY: Same job, I don't care when I do it.

FRANK: Good for you.

IZZY: The rest of the world should be so simple.

FRANK: Amen to that. They clink and drink.

IZZY: But you know what the thing is?

FRANK: What?

IZZY: With these dimmers. Who needs 'em anyway? The technology doesn't make anything better. You want atmosphere, light a candle. You know what I'm saying?

FRANK: Light a candle.

IZZY: Exactly.

FRANK: I like that.

IZZY: Cheers.

(They clink and drink.)

IZZY: So what do you got in the bag?

FRANK: Huh?

IZZY: Shopping or what's that?

FRANK: Oh yeah, just some stuff Gloria asked me to pick up. You know for the house and what not.

IZZY: Sure.

(Pause)

FRANK: So let me ask you this.

IZZY: Yeah?

FRANK: All those rich women you meet. Park Avenue, bored, alone, husband whatever.

IZZY: Yeah?

FRANK: They ever come on to you?

IZZY: How do you mean?

FRANK: Well, the cliche. You know. Electrical man comes into the apartment....

IZZY: You know what it is Frank? It's all in the vibes you put out.

FRANK: How's that?

IZZY: They can sense it. You want them to come onto you, "oh excuse me, will this take long, let me just slip into something a little more comfortable". I don't want that Frank. I don't need that. You don't put those vibes out there, you don't get them back.

FRANK: Makes sense.

IZZY: Sure. It's all in the vibes.

(Pause)

FRANK: I gotta pee.

(FRANK exits. IZZY sits for awhile. Sips his beer. Bored. He notices the shopping bag and decides to take a peek. He pulls out a plain looking box. He opens the box and removes a paddle, the kind one would use for an S & M spanking. He looks confused. Quickly he returns the paddle to the box and the box to the bag. FRANK re-enters.)

FRANK: Hey on Sunday for the game?

IZZY: Yeah?

FRANK: You think you could bring back my hedge cutters?

IZZY: Oh, sure. I'm sorry about that.

FRANK: No, it's no problem, it's just been a long time.

IZZY: I keep forgetting.

FRANK: No big thing, I just...you know it's time for a trim.

IZZY: No sweat. Sunday. You got it.

FRANK: Thanks, I appreciate it.

IZZY: Thank you for lending them to me.

FRANK: No problem.

IZZY: And for being so patient.

FRANK: Yeah. Whatever. You know. *(Pause)* So, let me ask you this.

IZZY: Yeah?

FRANK: Did you ever do anything for Cathy, like as a surprise, that you didn't think would go well and you were...I don't know afraid?

IZZY: Afraid? Hmm. I threw her a surprise party once.

FRANK: I remember. For her fiftieth.

IZZY: Scared the shit out of her.

FRANK: I still have that picture.

IZZY: "Surprise!" and she almost had a heart attack.

FRANK: That was a great party you threw.

IZZY: Yeah.

FRANK: Yeah. But I mean more like, you want to try something different and you just think, what if she doesn't like it?

IZZY: What, like in bed?

FRANK: Not necessarily.

IZZY: But with you?

FRANK: We're not talking about me. I'm asking you a question.

IZZY: Do we try different things in bed?

FRANK: No, I'm just asking if you ever tried something with Cathy that you thought maybe she wouldn't like.

IZZY: I took her whitewater rafting once. That was a disaster.

FRANK: I remember that too.

IZZY: She hates getting wet. What was I thinking?
Stayed mad at me for a week.

FRANK: O K, but I mean something more personal.

IZZY: Frank what are you driving at? You want to ask
me something, ask me something.

FRANK: I don't know. Skip it.

IZZY: No, what, go ahead. You can't talk to me, who
you gonna talk to?

FRANK: It's not worth getting into. Forget I brought it
up. Maybe it's not even worth doing.

(*Pause*)

IZZY: You know what it is Frank?

FRANK: What?

IZZY: I borrowed your clippers. I'm returning them late.
But you don't care, right? I don't have to say I'm sorry.
Because you know I didn't do it out of malice. No big
deal.

FRANK: So?

IZZY: So that's it.

FRANK: That's what?

IZZY: I don't know. Friendship. Love. Whatever.
You trust each other and that's it. As long as the other
person knows you're coming from the right place.
You try. You should try.

FRANK: Because why?

IZZY: Because...because if you stop trying you're fucked.

FRANK: How so?

IZZY: Trust me. I stopped trying for awhile. With Cathy.
Few years back. I just...stopped. It was like I was in a
zone.

FRANK: A zone?

IZZY: A numb zone of nothing.

FRANK: And?

IZZY: And she almost left me. You remember.

FRANK: Yeah. Yeah I do.

IZZY: That was the worst time of my life. I mean I was low. Don't do that Frank.

FRANK: It's hard though.

IZZY: It is hard. But it's the intentions that count....

FRANK: The intentions.

IZZY: ...not the results. Do you trust Gloria?

FRANK: Sure.

IZZY: Does she trust you?

FRANK: Of course.

IZZY: Then you have nothing to worry about.

FRANK: No? I mean, I wasn't worried. I was just asking a question. Making conversation. You know.

IZZY: Oh. O K. Well...good then, whatever.

(Pause)

FRANK: So you think I should.

IZZY: Should what?

FRANK: Whatever.

IZZY: I do. I think you more than should.

FRANK: But I do think change is scary.

IZZY: Sure. We love our routines. Fridays at O'Hanahans.

FRANK: Sunday games.

IZZY: Cards. I couldn't get out of bed without my routines.

FRANK: So change is scary.

IZZY: Change is scary.

FRANK: That's all I'm trying to say.

IZZY: Well said.

(Pause)

FRANK: You and Cathy always seem so happy together.

IZZY: Yeah, we're happy. You and Gloria too.

FRANK: Oh yeah, we are.

IZZY: You don't know what goes on behind closed doors. There's always something.

FRANK: Amen to that.

IZZY: That's just part of it.

(Pause)

FRANK: So do you know that I can't wait to go home to my wife?

IZZY: Yeah?

FRANK: Isn't that a nice feeling?

IZZY: Ah, the best.

FRANK: After all these years, and I still feel that way. When I married Gloria I thought she was so much better than me. Sometimes I forget that. But tonight. Tonight I'm going to change my life.

IZZY: What happens tonight?

FRANK: Ah, I don't know, nothing, you know, but just, tonight's gonna be a special night. I'm going to make it a special night.

IZZY: Good for you.

FRANK: I'm gonna make it special.

IZZY: It's up to you.

FRANK: Yeah. So, listen, I should head home.

IZZY: Yeah, me too.

FRANK: But I'm seeing you Sunday right?

IZZY: Sunday it is.

FRANK: And you won't forget the clippers?

IZZY: Won't forget.

(They get up to go.)

FRANK: Hey Izzy?

IZZY: Yeah?

FRANK: Thanks a lot for talking to me.

IZZY: No problem, that's what friends are for.

FRANK: We said a lot didn't we?

IZZY: Yes we did Frank. I think in the course of one beer, we pretty much said it all.

(Lights fade to black.)

END OF PLAY